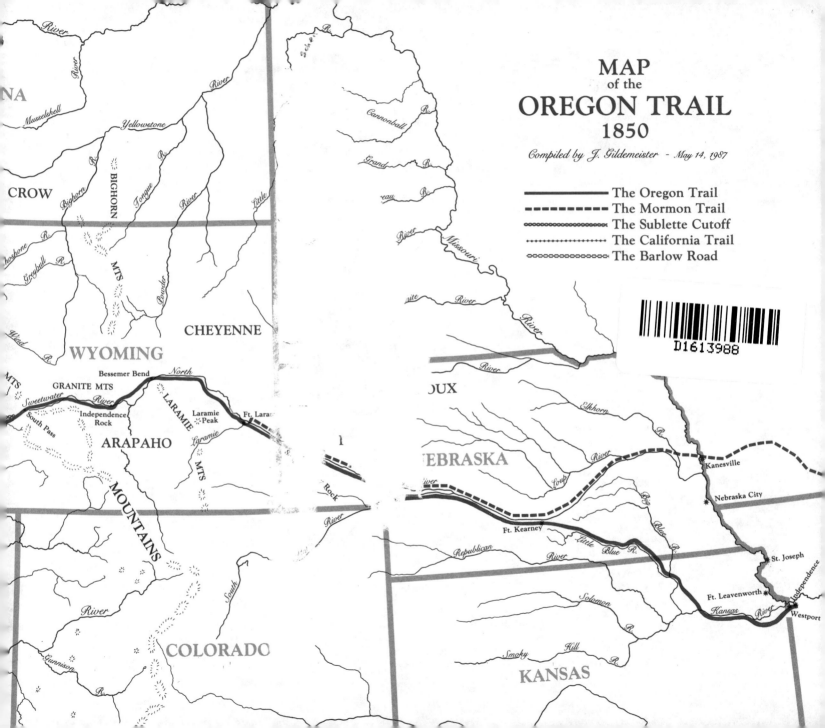

MAP
of the
OREGON TRAIL
1850

Compiled by J. Gildemeister - May 14, 1987

─────────	The Oregon Trail
─ ─ ─ ─ ─	The Mormon Trail
◦◦◦◦◦◦◦◦	The Sublette Cutoff
············	The California Trail
⬭⬭⬭⬭⬭⬭	The Barlow Road

D1613988

NA

Musselshell

River

Yellowstone

River

CROW

Bighorn

BIGHORN

Tongue

River

Little

River

BIGHORN MTS

Shoshone R.

Greybull R.

Wind R.

Powder

River

CHEYENNE

WYOMING

Cannonball R.

Grand R.

eau R.

River

Missouri

River

ute River

River

OUX

IOUX

Elkhorn

R.

NEBRASKA

River

Loup

River

Big

Kanesville

Nebraska City

Bessemer Bend

North

GRANITE MTS

Sweetwater

River

Independence
Rock

South Pass

MTS

LARAMIE

Laramie
Peak

Ft. Laram

ARAPAHO

Laramie

MTS

MOUNTAINS

River

South

River

COLORADO

Gunnison

R.

Rock

River

Ft. Kearney

Republican

River

Little Blue R.

Blue

R.

Solomon

Kansas

River

Smoky

Hill

R.

KANSAS

St. Joseph

Ft. Leavenworth

Independence

Westport

A
Limited
First Printing

Jerry Gildemeister

Don Gray

We reached the Sweetwater, traveling through a naked, bleak country, the bare granite rocks lifting their craggy heads above the sea of sand and sandstone....

John Ball - 1852

Ezra Meeker resting along the Oregon Trail

A Letter Home

Text, Design & Photographic Illustration by Gildemeister
Historical Narratives by Lucia Williams and Other Pioneers
Original Art by Don Gray

About the Book

One might ask — why another book about the Oregon Trail? Hundreds of books have been written about the pioneer journey to the American West. In fact, it was just seven years ago that The Bear Wallow produced *Traces*, stories of the last still-living pioneers who traveled by covered wagon over the Oregon Trail. When we realized there were pioneers still alive who traveled by covered wagon over the Trail, we were compelled to do their story.

Today, nearly all - if not all - the Oregon Trail Pioneers have passed on. They are no longer able to give first-hand accounts of their adventures. All that remains are the personal letters, diaries, and remnants of the Trail as a testimonial to their struggles of traveling 2,000 miles over the wild, desolate country.

What was it like to pack all of your belongings, leave behind family and friends, and head out in a covered wagon on an unknown 2,000 mile journey beset with untold difficulties, misery, and dangers? And, all this in the mid-1800's, when there were no towns along the way to seek provisions, repairs or shelter...no medical station for accident or illness...and no law enforcement in case of danger or attack.

A letter written in 1851 by Lucia Lorain Williams was recently brought to our attention; it answers some of these questions and gave us the inspiration for 'one more book' on the Oregon Trail. It is such a unique letter in the sense that it reads more like a novel — with grand descriptions of one family's westward adventure during the heyday of the migration to the Oregon Country. To support the letter, we have relied on the diary of E. W. Conyers and the writings of Ezra Meeker — both of whom traveled the Trail in 1852.

4

To complement the writings, extensive journeys were made during the period of 1979 through 1986, locating remnants of the Trail in pristine condition and photographing — as much as man's development allows — to depict the countryside much as the pioneers would have witnessed it more than a century ago.

Illustration for Lucia Williams' letter is original artwork by Don Gray. There is little significant photographic documentation in the early days of the Trail, so historic photos of later decades have been used on the assumption that the pioneers did not change much during those years; only their mode of transportation switched from oxen to horses and mules.

A Letter Home is divided into three parts, opening with *The Pioneer Journey* of leaving family and friends behind, crossing the Missouri, and heading out in covered wagons across wild Indian Country — traveling westward to the Continental Divide and over South Pass into *The Land of Promise* — The Oregon Country. The journey west of the Rocky Mountains was a struggle to cross dry deserts and treacherous rivers to reach the Willamette Valley of Oregon before winter storms blocked the mountain passes. The final chapter is *A Letter Home*, Lucia Williams' letter to her mother, describing the family's adventurous journey to Oregon in 1851. Our postscript, historical notes, and related material finish the book.

Lastly, we dedicate this book to the memory of all the Oregon Trail Pioneers. We hope that *A Letter Home* serves to amplify the significance of the Oregon Trail and the sacrifices made by these pioneers in claiming the West for America.

Prologue

It is hard to comprehend that less than two lifetimes ago the area west of the Continental Divide, known as the Oregon Country, was a huge wilderness inhabited only by Indians and small groups of Hudson's Bay Company trappers, a handful of traders, and a scant number of American mountain men.

In the early 1800s the Oregon Country encompassed the present states of Washington, Oregon, Idaho, as well as a portion of Wyoming, Montana, and Western Canada. The British and the French had laid claim to this vast territory, and most Americans showed little interest in the area...not until the Lewis and Clark expedition of 1804-06 to explore the Louisiana Territory and seek a trade route to the Pacific.

This expedition served to enhance the United States claim to the Pacific Northwest. In 1818, the United States and Great Britain entered into a treaty calling for joint occupation of the Oregon Country. The massive western migration of emigrants to Oregon in the early 1840s clinched the United States claim to the Pacific Northwest. This nearly led to war, but the treaty of 1846 established the boundary between Canada and the United States at the 49th parallel.

Today, with air travel commonplace and the country intersected with high-speed roads, few have any concept of that 2000 mile journey by covered wagon...traveling 10 to 15 miles each day with little protection from torrential rains, baking sun, and freezing winds...and the misery, difficulties, and dangers that awaited the pioneers along the Oregon Trail.

Of the early travelers, some were seeking to escape the nation's financial collapse of 1837 and the depression to follow, some sought to escape the dreaded epidemics of sickness and the foul industrial air of the cities, while others wanted to escape religious persecution. A mass movement of feverish fortune seekers followed in 1849, the year after the first gold strike in California. Slightly more than a decade later, the American Civil War caused another wave of migration westward to escape the war's devastation. All were searching for a better life out West; and all were to share similar experiences on the longest pioneer road in history.

As a highway of travel, the Oregon Trail was the most remarkable. It was a route with no sign of civilization except for four trading posts and an occasional trader's cabin between the landings on the Missouri and Fort Vancouver on the Columbia. The Trail originated with the use of travelers — no surveyor ever located a foot of it nor ever established a grade; no engineer sought out a water crossing nor built a bridge; there was practically no surfacing to the road bed; and, considering the era, the quality of this two thousand mile highway was remarkably good.

But the Trail could also be one of the worst ever traveled. When spring rains came, travel was slow or at a standstill in the mud. Streambeds that usually could be forded ran torrents of water. When prairies became dry and parched, the road filled with stifling dust...waterholes dried, became alkaline and unfit to drink. The summer sun poured down with such intensity that lips cracked, skin burned, and wagon wheels dried and fell apart. Sudden snowstorms in the mountains sometimes caught the travelers unprepared, and there was more misery and suffering. Along with that came sickness from exposure and overexertion, and death from the dreaded cholera. It was then that the trail became a highway of desolation — strewn with abandoned goods, broken wagons, the skeletons of oxen, horses and mules — and the freshly made mounds that told the pitiful tale of the suffering encountered on the westward journey.

There was no register of travelers over the Oregon Trail, no accurate count of those left along the wayside; but existing records indicate more than half a million emigrants passed over the Trail between 1843 and the last days of its use when highways and the automobile brought about its demise.

All that is left today are scattered remnants of the Trail itself, undisturbed by the hand of man, and the dusted remains of over 30,000 souls who perished along the way.

*I find that the best place to fit out is at Independence — oxen
can be had at 25$ pr yoke — mules & horses from 30 to 40$
pr head — flour this year 4$ per bbl....*

George McKinstry - May 21, 1846

The Pioneer Journey

It was a sight long to be remembered — hundreds of covered wagons lined up at the river landings.

They had come from near and far. Some were city dwellers and others were farmers converging on the portals of the West — Independence Landing, Westport, Ft. Leavenworth, St. Joseph, Nebraska City, and Kanesville...these were the Oregon Trail pioneers.

Even though much of the land across Iowa and Missouri was quite flat, the roads leading here were running mud, caused by the spring rains and the concentrated travel of oxen pulling wagons heavily loaded with all the earthly goods of the pioneers. And there were more wagons coming everyday. Many of the roads were so bad that mud oozed ahead of the wagon's fore axle, forcing a stop every few minutes for the stock to rest.

Oxen were generally favored over horses and mules for the trip across the Plains for they were better for pulling through mud and fording streams. The Indians could not run them off at night as easily as they could horses; and, once at their destination, the oxen were easier to care for and far better at breaking up vast stretches of sod.

At the landings there was much excitement among the pioneers anxious to be on their way. Here on the Missouri last minute provisions were obtained, harness and tack was repaired, and the last letters were written and sent back to family and friends, for there would be little chance to write and few places to post a letter for the next four to six months — not until they got to their destination, nearly 2000 miles away.

The greater body of emigrants formed themselves into large companies and elected captains to lead the group westward. The independent and smaller parties planned to travel close together for there was safety in numbers — and there was someone to help in time of need.

We started on our way; we came about four miles and sank fast in the mud up to our axles. Our load consisted of bedding, clothing and provisions, weighed about 1,600 pounds all told. All this we were obliged to unload before we could extricate our wagon....

E.W. Conyers - April 21, 1852

Once the emigrants set foot on the other side of the Missouri they were in Indian country, where no organized civil government existed. The law of preservation asserted itself, and the counsels of levelheaded older men prevailed. When occasion called for action, a high court was convened. From necessity, murder was punishable by death. The penalty for stealing was a severe whipping. Minor offenses or differences, generally, were arbitrated—each party abiding by the decision as if it had been handed down from a court of law.

Usually it was mid-May before there was sufficient grass on the Plains to permit travel west of the Missouri. Some wise emigrants started early and fed grain until the grass was green enough to sustain the stock.

A loud whistle blast announced the arrival of the first steamer and the opening of the river to westward travel. Emigrants rushed to the landing to book passage. A dozen or more wagons could be carried across the river at one time by steamer, and at least a dozen trips could be made during the day, with as many more at night. Passage ran $10 per wagon with four yoke of oxen, and $2 for every extra yoke.

If a scow was available, two more wagons could make the crossing. The price was only $4 per wagon, but the cattle would have to swim in the swift current.

West of the Missouri the whitemen would be trespassing across land of the Pawnee and the Sioux. This was their hunting ground and their home. It was a land sacred to them.

Trouble soon started for the pioneers, not from the Indian, but from their own indiscretion. The rush to get ahead of the traveling throng caused teams to break down. Wagons loaded with a ton of provisions sank in bottomland mud. At stream crossings, when heavy wagons bogged down, the pioneers were forced to unload and backpack their belongings across to the other side, causing a general outcry against all of the unnecessary articles.

First to be cast out might be a table or cupboard, or perhaps a bedstead, a cast-iron cookstove, or extra bedding. Then there would be entire wagons and their provisions — sacks of flour and sides of bacon being the most abundant — all left as common property. Along the trail were hundreds of wagons with hundreds of tons of goods. Anyone could help themselves. People seemed to vie with each other in giving away their property as there was no chance to sell anything, and they disliked destroying the goods.

In the early days the pioneers started from Independence and Westport, following the Santa Fe Trail for roughly forty miles through the Kansas country before turning northwest for the Oregon Country. Travel over these low plains was generally favorable with fifteen to twenty miles considered a good day's drive.

Large game was already scarce, for here on the low plain the buffalo were gone and only an occasional deer was seen near thickets along the streams.

Grass and water were good and wood was abundant in the drainage bottoms, but there was always the threat of sudden, violent storms which would swell the streams and make crossings dangerous. The Kansas River had to be ferried by using rafts constructed of two canoes overlaid with a platform of poles. It was with great difficulty and exertion that wagons were lowered down the steep riverbank to the raft. The stock was forced to swim in the rapid, turbid current and then exert themselves to pull the wagons up the other bank.

It was a four day trip to Alcove Spring on the east side of the Big Blue River. There the travelers would find good water and an excellent campsite surrounded by ash, cottonwood, and cedar.

After crossing the Big Blue the trail led over open, grassy hills spotted with an occasional scattering of trees. The wagons paralleled the Little Blue all the way to the breaks, and then headed toward Grand Island on the Platte River.

Emigrant Encampment

Some one of our camp makes daily trips to the different ferry
landings to see what chance there will be for us to cross the
Missouri River and resume our trip across the continent....
                    E.W. Conyers - May 9, 1852

After 1846 another route of the pioneers was along the Mormon Trail which crossed the Mississippi and Des Moines rivers heading to Kanesville, Iowa—later known as Council Bluffs. Here they crossed the Missouri and traveled west on the north side of the Platte. Like the travel along the Oregon Trail to the south, this led over low plains of bountiful grass and abundant wood along the stream bottoms. The trail led across the Elkhorn River, Shell Creek, the Loup Fork of the Platte, Wood River, and Elm Creek before continuing along the north bank of the Platte to the Fort Laramie crossing.

We observe that the emigrants are digging wells in the low lands
for water, which they obtain by digging from eight to ten feet, rather
than drink the muddy water of the Platte. We were advised not to
drink this water, as it is strongly impregnated with alkali....
                    E.W. Conyers - May 25, 1852

A post, first named Fort Childs and then Fort Kearney, was located on the south side of the Platte near the head of Grand Island.

The fort was an open post of sod and adobe structures, notoriously uncomfortable, but a busy and important post. This was the first chance since crossing the Missouri for pioneers to post letters back to families in the East.

Here, too, was the nesting place of the Sandhill Crane. A place with glorious sunsets and the silhouette of thousands of birds returning in the nighttime sky.

We started this morning at 6 o'clock. Roads are very heavy and sandy. We came seven miles in the forenoon. Roads not so bad this afternoon. Came twenty miles today and camped on Prairie Creek. No wood and water not good....

E.W. Conyers - May 31, 1852

Tonight we are obliged to obtain our woods from an island,
wading in the water about three feet deep. Grass very scarce; all
been eaten off within two miles of our camp....

E.W. Conyers - June 5, 1852

This was the beginning of the high plains. The tall grass prairies were giving way to more arid, desert-like country with sandy soils marked with yucca, buffalo grass, and low cactus. Cottonwood and willows were abundant on the river islands. Ash and cedar were found in coves and canyons beyond the bluffs that paralleled the broad valley bottom.

Buffalo were to be found in great numbers, and fresh meat was easily obtainable for those wishing to risk using horses in the chase over a score of prairie-dog towns. Antelope were also plentiful, as were rattlesnakes and wolves.

Stream crossings remained difficult for the pioneers because the sandy, fluid bottom required great exertion of energy to pull the wagons through.

At times the dust was intolerable. In calm weather it would rise so thickly that often the lead team of oxen could not be seen from the wagon. Then again, heavy winds would blow the sand with enough force to sting the face and nearly blind both man and beast.

Sometimes the pioneers would be caught in sudden cloudbursts that would wet them to the skin in no time. Some camps were severly damaged by the fury of the wind and rain when sheets of water carried off camp equipment, ox yokes, and any other loose items left on the ground.

Sound of the violin and merrymaking has been seldom heard during the past week, and pleasure has given way to mourning and lamentation and many new-made graves are to be seen by the roadside as we pass along...This afternoon we saw our first buffalo. It was across the river on the south side of the Platte....

E.W. Conyers - June 13, 1852

Plains Buffalo

Found a family consisting of husband, wife, and four small children, whose cattle we supposed had given out and died. They were here all alone, and no wagon in sight....
Unknown Pioneer - 1852

Water from the Platte was comparatively pure, except for the sediment, so fine, seemingly held in solution; pioneers often dug small wells along the banks of the river, but they were heavily charged with alkali. Between the bad water from the wells and the unsanitary conditions all along the trail, the result was great sickness to the emigrants and their stock alike, ultimately affecting even the native inhabitants. It is little wonder that the Indians became extremely dangerous and unfriendly to the whiteman.

In the early days of the trail, the only threat from the Pawnee and the Sioux was the nuisance of begging and occasional theft of stock. As the emigration increased, the wagons frightened the buffalo away; and the grassland and wood supply was destroyed along the river valley. Cholera and other sickness spread like wildfire and the Indian tribes were decimated.

The Pawnee numbers were halved by the spread of disease from their contact with the whiteman. The Sioux began attacking wagon trains to rid their land of the emigrants until 1851, when a treaty was signed at Fort Laramie to permit wagon trains to have free access of travel.

New hazards and problems awaited the travelers as they moved westward. Heavy pulling was required in the sandy hills and over steep grades. The drier climate helped make the heat of day more bearable from the muggy weather along the Missouri, but it caused wood wheels to shrink and become rickety. The worst problem was the lack of firewood to alleviate the chill of evening, or to dry out after the frequent thunderstorms. The only things left for the cooking fire were buffalo chips.

The first really imposing land barrier along the emigrant road was the climb from the South Platte, up California Hill, over the ridge, and the steep descent down Windlass Hill to the bottom of Ash Creek, a deep ravine which runs into the North Platte. This was the first steep ground encountered by the pioneers. Their ingenuity and skill were tested in the process of pulling up one side of the hill and lowering the wagons with rope and chains down the other side to Ash Hollow. Here was a favorite spot for resting and refitting in the shade of ash trees. Though food was scant, there was the luxury of clear, cold springs and abundant firewood. The pioneers were 500 miles out and a quarter of the way to their destination.

After a brief rest, they continued their journey westward along the hot, dry river bottom, past the sentinels of the North Platte — Courthouse Rock, Jail Rock, Chimney Rock, and Scotts Bluff. All were so prominent on the skyline and so unique in shape, that nearly all diarists traveling the trail noted their existence.

The original route of the Oregon Trail led away from the Platte to Robidoux Pass, south of Scotts Bluff. Far to the west was Laramie Peak, a prominent mountain that would be a visual landmark to the traveler for days to come.

After 1848 a shorter route was located through the pass at Scotts Bluff. The trail led through desolate dry country that was full of sand, little grass, and no firewood, so buffalo chips were at a premium to supply the cooking fires.

The two routes led over the Laramie Plain to combine at Horse Creek. The trapper-missionary-Mormon trail paralleled along the north bank of the Platte. All were passing through the land of the Cheyenne and Arapaho.

It was along this stretch of the trail that cholera took more of a toll than anywhere else.

The sick and the dying are on the right, on the left, in front and in the rear, and in our midst. Death is behind as well as before. Many are stalking their way through pestilence unmoved, while others view each step with perfect consternation....

John Wood - 1850

At 650 miles out, the Oregon Trail crossed the Laramie River and the Mormon Trail crossed the North Platte to link-up at Fort Laramie, the gateway to the Rocky Mountains. The fort, with adobe walls six feet thick and fifteen feet high, topped with wooded palisades, was built in 1841 by the American Fur Company and originally called Fort John. Emigrants found this post could usually provide essential supplies, blacksmithing, and wagon repair.

Except for those who stopped at Fort Kearney, this was the first point to post a letter since leaving the Missouri.

During the ox-team days of the early 1850s, when the migration was at its peak, the army of pioneers out of Fort Laramie made an unbroken column fully five hundred miles long.

Counted as many as 500 graves along the North Platte....
Sickness lasted usually but a day. Many with beds and blankets
were abandoned by the roadside, and no man, not even an Indian,
dared touch them, for fear of the unknown, unseen destroyer....
Oscar Hyde - May 2, 1850

I carried a little motherless babe five hundred miles, whose
mother had died, and when we would camp I would go from camp
to camp in search of some good, kind, motherly woman to let it
nurse, and no one ever refused when I presented it to them....
                                              Margaret W. Inman - 1852

The animals driven over the Plains during this period were also legend. Besides those that labored under yoke, in harness, and under saddle, there was a vast herd of loose stock — hundreds of thousands in fact.

Is it any wonder the old trail was worn so deep that in places it looked like a canal? Within a days travel west of Fort Laramie, the pioneers paused to inscribe a record of their passing in the soft sandstone of Register Cliff. Here the road cut six feet deep in solid sandstone is a testament to the thousands of wagons heading west.

One wonders how deep this cut would have been if all the travel was over this route, since a great many followed the hill route to the south.

The Oregon Trail at Register Rock

We crossed N. fork of the Platte & left it immediately.
It was quite small. We saw it no more....

Rev. Parrish -1843

As the column filed up the North Platte, there was some relief from the dust. The throng was visibly thinned out; some had pushed on ahead, while others had lagged behind. The dead, too, had left room on the road, as it is estimated for every day's travel of fifteen miles, 250 souls were buried along the trail—totaling over 30,000 that never reached their intended destination.

Mirages were commonplace on the prairie—images of scenes that the pioneers thought were close at hand. They saw sheets of water so real as to be almost within their grasp, but never touched, hills and valleys they would never traverse, and beautiful scenes on a horizon never reached.

Ahead lay the last crossing of the North Platte. Emigrants not fording at the lower crossing left the river behind at the trapper crossing of Bessemer Bend and the Red Buttes.

The routes joined again at Poison Spring and continued west over the desolate rolling terrain sparse with water except for alkali lakes and sloughs until the Sweetwater River was reached.

The nights were cooler and the Sweetwater was clear and pure. At times, the hordes of insects were intolerable. The buzz of mosquitoes could be heard long before they were seen in large, black swarms, and no-see-ums attacked the heads of man and beast to inflict painful bites until escape was made only by retreating to higher ground.

Here along the Sweetwater was Independence Rock, a distinctive turtle or whale-shaped rock of solid granite, rising out of the flat valley bottom.

Not much water for the cattle...grass not good. Quite a number of cattle in our company are getting lame by traveling over hot, sandy and stony roads....
E.W. Conyers - June 30, 1852

From here we had a splendid view of the surrounding country for miles. We found the rock literally covered with the names of emigrants....

E.W. Conyers - July 2, 1852

Independence Rock was named by mountain men on the Fourth of July in commemoration of the Nation's birthday. By far, the monument is the most famous along the entire Oregon Trail. It served as a wilderness 'post office' for travelers to look for messages from friends ahead or to leave for those yet to come.

Thousands of emigrants, traders, and trappers climbed the rock for a grand view of the surrounding countryside and inscribed their names for posterity. And many a traveler made a special effort to camp here on the 4th of July to celebrate this momentous occasion.

The train was occupied by an unbroken column 500 miles long, that at 15 miles a day it would take a month for that column to pass this point....

Ezra Meeker - 1852

Names scribed into Independence Rock

Shoshoni, Arapaho, Crow, and Sioux shared the Sweetwater valley before the area became heavily traveled by the emigrants and traders. Their hunting pattern, culture, and lifestyle were changed forever. Friction between the tribes and the newcomers from the East led to tragic warfare and loss to the Indians of this grand country they had known as theirs.

As the emigrants ascended the Sweetwater, life became more tolerable with good water and cooler nights. They guided on Devils Gate, with the trail heading over a low pass of the Rattlesnake Mountains. Here was another favorite camping site where the Sweetwater ran between vertical rock walls.

It was yet another stop to bury the dead.

About a dozen burnt wagons and nineteen dead oxen were passed today along the road; but the destruction has not been by no means as great as upon the North Fork of the Platte and the crossing over the Sweetwater....

Capt. Howard Stansbury - August 1, 1852

The Resting Place of T. P. Baker at Devils Gate

Since I wrote we have passed Devil's Gate, crossed the Sweetwater five times, and now ascending the Rocky Mountains, and in two days will get our first sight of Oregon.....Mary lost one of her oxen, one of the best. It could ill be spared....

Agnes Stewart - July 12, 1853

A days travel westward took them to Split Rock, a cleft in the top of the Rattlesnake Range that was a famous natural landmark used by Indians, trappers, and emigrants on the Oregon Trail.

Their passage up the Sweetwater was barren of good grass. Here the vegetation changed to greasewood, creosotebush, and sagebrush, with the sage being the principle source of firewood. The erosion of the surrounding barren ridges caused an accumulation of dusty alkali deposits and bitter waters. Such irritants were hard on people and livestock, and great care had to be taken to avoid loss of animals from alkali poisoning.

The bleached bones of cattle, horses, and mules were scattered all along the Sweetwater — victims of exhaustion, lameness, and the alkali.

In the early days of emigration through the Sweetwater Valley, buffalo could be found and antelope were common. Elk, grizzly bear, and wolves lived in the surrounding hills, and a large population of coyotes could always be heard in their search for ground squirrels and jackrabbits.

The climb to the crest of the continent was not over a treacherous mountain pass as many supposed, but only a gradual climb to the summit of the Rockies. The trail led through South Pass, the gateway to the Oregon Country. The pioneers were nearly halfway to their destination as they passed through this wide open, undulating country covered with sagebrush.

The Land of Promise

Today we set foot in Oregon Territory... 'the land of promise' as yet only promises an increased supply of wormwood and sand....

Theodore Talbot - August 22, 1843

Far to the north were the snowcapped Wind River Mountains rising over 13,000 feet in height. The emigrants were at 7,550 feet on the Continental Divide with the route heading downhill to the Pacific shores.

The surrounding area was a middle ground for the Indian tribes. Hunting excursions were made by Sioux, Cheyenne, and Arapaho from the east; Crow and Gros Ventres from the north; Shoshoni and Bannocks from the west; and Utes from the south. War parties often took horses and scalps, but the emigrants suffered less here from thievery than they had on the Great Plains, and were less prone to attacks than in the Snake River Valley that faced them to the west.

The trail led past Pacific Springs, down the Big Sandy. Scorching days were frequently followed by freezing nights. Feed was sparse and water holes were often of alkali, all the way to Green River.

Eighteen miles west of South Pass, just beyond Dry Sandy crossing, the pioneers reached the 'Parting of the Ways', a split in the trail westward. To the left was Fort Bridger and the Mormon Road to the Great Salt Lake; to the right was the Sublette Cutoff — a route saving the traveler nearly 50 miles to the Bear Valley, but they were 50 waterless miles. Either way, travelers on both routes had to make the Green River crossing.

We found our way into the river bottom
by a precipitous and difficult descent from
the top of a very high bluff....
  James A. Pritchard - June 21, 1849

The Green was a good resting spot with ample water and welcome shade of cottonwoods lining the river bottom. But all was not good, as it was also the first water barrier on the western slope. Pioneers used several routes looking for a good crossing, but the Green could be forded only before the spring runoff or late in the summer when the water level was at its ebb. At all other times wagons had to be ferried across and the stock forced to swim in the fast current.

To the west was the Little Colorado Desert, another stretch of rough hills and wasteland to negotiate before the Rockies were left behind and relief attained along the Bear River. Those choosing the route to Fort Bridger could obtain some essential supplies or blacksmithing, and there was a chance to exchange worn-out stock for serviceable animals. From Fort Bridger, the Oregon Trail pioneers left the Mormon Trail and headed northwest to join their fellow travelers who used the Sublette Cutoff to the Bear Valley.

Along the Bear River a most unusual natural phenomenon greeted the travelers at Soda Springs. Right in the middle of the river, Steamboat Spring spouted at regular intervals as the wagons passed. At Soda Point the Bear River turned to the south and a trail to California went with it. The Hudspeth Cutoff to California headed west to the Raft River route. The Oregon Trail continued northwest through the wide valley to Fort Hall, the stockaded trading post built by Nathaniel Wyeth in 1834 on the east bank of the Snake River. The fort was sold to the Hudson's Bay Company in 1837 and rebuilt the next year with white adobe walls to become an important way-station on the trail until it was abandoned in 1856 due to the increasing hostilities of the Shoshoni and Bannock Indians who saw their river pastures destroyed and their people decimated by the whiteman's diseases.

Five miles to the north, Fort Hall, with its white-washed walls, is plainly in view. The 'Three Buttes' rise in the distance, while the Port Neuf, with its bright sparkling waters, flows at our feet....

Howard Stansbury - August, 1844

Could easily hear the sound of a waterfall...much surprise to learn the next day that within ten miles of this place there is a cascade which is not surpassed by the Niagara falls....

Unknown Pioneer - August 15, 1849

From Fort Hall the trail led down the south bank of the Snake to American Falls, a series of low falls cascading over compressed ridges of basalt rock, a landmark and favorite camping place for the emigrants.

Farther on the wagons stopped at Register Rock where pioneers camped and again left their mark for posterity. Another days travel brought them to the Raft River crossing and another division of the trail. This was the start of the California Trail which headed southwest to the Humboldt River — carrying travelers over the High Sierras to California, the same trail used by the Applegates in 1847 in their search for a southern route to Oregon.

The Oregon Trail continued along the south shore of the Snake, through lava outcroppings, sparse grass and sagebrush, and scattered juniper — a most inhospitable land, as game was scarce and the Indians considered treacherous.

Within earshot of the trail was Shoshoni Falls, a magnificent view of a giant cataract cascading down two hundred feet into the Snake River gorge. Not many stopped to visit, but those who did never regretted delay.

Here again the heat became oppressive, the dust stifling, and the thirst at times maddening. In places the pioneers could see the water of the Snake winding through lava gorges, but they couldn't reach it, as the river ran in the inaccessible depths of the canyon. Sickness again became prevalent, and another outbreak of cholera claimed many victims.

At Rock Creek a natural trail afforded the only possible crossing, as vertical walls of lava rock nearly a hundred feet in height boarded both sides of the stream.

We were obliged to descend a very rough, rocky and steep hill to reach the river, not knowing if we would be able to get our cattle back up the hill or not...it is so steep and bad that many cattle are too weak to climb the hill, therefore are left at the foot of the hill to perish among the big basalt boulders that cover the narrow bottoms of the Snake River....

E.W. Conyers - August 5, 1852

Another long day of travel brought them within view of Thousand Springs, a giant cascade of water gushing out of the rocks on the north bank of the Snake. The view was so impressive that it was recorded in many diaries.

Close by, at Salmon Falls, the emigrants could barter with the Indians for fish, a welcome change in their diet, as provisions were beginning to be depleted for many of the travelers.

Some emigrants made the decision to cross the Snake to get away from the desolate trail along the south bank of the river. There were no good fords and few ferries available. When they did exist, the charges were too high for most emigrants to afford, as many had exhausted their funds in outfitting for the journey westward— and few ever dreamed there would be use for money on the Plains, where there were neither supplies nor settlements.

A commonly used route across the river was at Three Island Crossing, though it was always dangerous and only fordable in low-water periods. From the north bank the trail headed northwest to the Boise River and the last crossing of the Snake at Fort Boise. The fort was built at the mouth of the Boise River by the Hudson's Bay Company and operated until it was flooded out in 1853.

Some who could not afford the expensive ferriage attempted to cross the river by disassembling their wagons, caulking the boxes, and floating across. Needless to say, they had no idea the treachery of the mighty Snake, and they lost everything they owned. Some even lost their lives in the process.

After terrible hardships, the survivors reached the road again, and were forced to eat only berries and insects until they could become recipients of charity from their fellow travelers.

To Snake River - crossed very deep to hind wheels - 7 yoke to a wagon...
Samuel Parker - August 14, 1845

Wagon Pioneers

From the Fort Boise crossing, some of the worst travel yet faced the pioneers. There were over 300 miles of dry desert, rocky canyons, steep hills, and rugged mountains before they would reach The Dalles or the Willamette Valley. It became a serious question with many: whether they had sufficient provisions to keep from starvation and whether their teams could muster strength enough to get them through. Everything that could possibly be spared was cast out to lighten loads, and many a wagon was left by the wayside when stock gave out. Only precious provisions and irreplaceable personal possessions were saved.

As the wagons pulled away from the Snake and headed northwest toward the Malheur River the dust got deeper every day. Often it would lie in the road a full six inches deep, so fine that a person wading through it would scarcely leave a track — it flowed just like water, and when disturbed, clouds would billow up to choke every breathing thing.

Two days travel later the wagons were back on the Snake at Farewell Bend. This was their last campsite at the river they had been companion with since leaving Fort Hall, some 330 miles back. Ahead of them lay the steep and rocky Burnt River Canyon — some of the worst terrain the emigrants would face since crossing the Missouri. Teams were often doubled to pull wagons up the steep, rocky grades. After traveling over miles of sagebrush and juniper-covered hills, the pioneers were at the top of Flagstaff Hill and one of the grandest views along the entire trail.

Three miles to Snake River...here the river turns to the right, and we bid farewell to the Snake River as we see it no more...

David Dinwiddie - August 19, 1853

(overleaf) Elkhorn Range of the Blue Mountains

To the northeast were the snowcapped Wallowa Mountains, and to the west, towering above the Powder Valley, lay the rugged Elkhorn Range of the Blue Mountains.

The trail led down Flagstaff Hill and traversed the expansive valley floor, crossed the Powder River, and then climbed to a timbered ridge of pine and fir. Ahead lay the steep, rugged descent into the Valley of the Grande Ronde. Logs had to be cut from standing trees and chained to the wagons to slow the descent, a drop of nearly 1300 feet, into the valley below.

From the mountain rim was another magnificent sight — a beautiful green valley surrounded by a circle of mountains. The valley had long been used by the Cayuse, Umatilla, and the Nez Perce Indians for hunting and gathering of roots. In spring the valley bottom was a lush green carpet of grass and rush with solid blue fields of Camas. Near the southern entrance to the valley were hot springs favored by whitemen and Indian alike. Many emigrants wished they could have stayed in the Grande Ronde, but it was late in the year. They had neither sufficient food nor money to take up stakes, and were forced to continue on to the Willamette Valley.

A short rest was all they could afford, since winter would soon be in the Blues and it would be a struggle to get over the mountains.

For some emigrants traveling late in the year, and those needing provisions or emergency help, Nez Perce Indians were often available to guide the wagons north to the Whitman Mission on the Walla Walla River.

After the spread of disease among the Indians, the Cayuse thought the Mission was the source of the epidemic that was killing their people, which prompted the Whitman Massacre of 1847 and the burning of the mission. After that the pioneers would have to travel another 180 miles to The Dalles before they would find any sign of civilization.

*This brought us to the summit of the mountain, overlooking the
Grande Ronde Valley, one of the prettiest and most welcome sights seen
on the whole route. Two miles more down a long steep and rocky road
brought us into the valley...*

E.W. Conyers - August 28, 1852

The Trail over the Blue Mountains

From the Valley of the Grande Ronde the pioneers started their long climb up the mountain, across open ridges, and down to cross the Grande Ronde River. Ahead they faced another tough climb to the top of the Blue Mountains. The trail passed through towering pines over a carpet of grass. Water at Emigrant Springs was good, so the pioneers often stayed over to rest up before the long descent of Emigrant Hill to the valley floor.

Those who traveled late in the year faced freezing temperatures and deep snow through the dense forest. It was a struggle to get across the Blues and down to the valley of the Umatilla Indians before winter winds would close the pass.

We started at 7 a.m. and traveled fifteen miles to the foot of the Blue Mountains. There is a fine spring at this camp, but no grass. The Indians have so many ponies herded in this vicinity that they eat the grass clean as they go....

E.W. Conyers - September 1, 1852

The route headed west across the Umatilla River. From here the travel was harsh across hills and flats of the dry Columbia Plain.

Those who visited the Whitman Mission either floated down the Columbia or continued by wagon over the dry, sterile land following the south bank of the Columbia to rejoin the main route heading west.

Firewood was scarce and so was water and feed for the stock. The route paralleled the flow of the Columbia — across Butter Creek and Sand Hollow to Well Spring, and then across Willow Creek, the John Day, and finally to the awesome Columbia. Here Indians settlements lined the river banks, and the natives were always on hand to help in the river portage at Celilo Falls or with the wagon crossings of the Deschutes River.

The land route climbed nearly a thousand feet up and then headed over the ridge to The Dalles. On top the pioneers witnessed an inspiring view of snowcapped Mt. Hood looming on the skyline.

Here we forded the John Day River and traveled down the river one-half mile and camped....A woman died, a few minutes ago, in the next train to our camp. About five or six days since she gave birth to a child, and traveling over tough roads in her condition was too much for her....

E.W. Conyers - September 9, 1852

Within a day they had reached The Dalles, and the end of the Oregon Trail.
Here the portage ground was thick with emigrant families — their clothes, shoes,
bodies, stock, and wagons worn out from the long, grueling journey.

Nearing Journey's End

All were waiting for passage down the Columbia. Some would give up their stock to pay their way while others were able to keep their teams and wagons for use at their destination. The river travelers were faced with another barrier at Cascade Locks where Indians again helped with the portage. The trip from The Dalles to Fort Vancouver took from four days to two weeks, but the pioneers were treated with the beauty of the Columbia Gorge—towering rock pillars, dense forests, and cascading waterfalls—all beautiful, inspirational sights.

Some with wagons would disembark at the Sandy River to continue the overland route up the Willamette Valley. All others would travel to Fort Vancouver and then up the Willamette River by boat and raft until the 1850s when travelers were blessed with steamboat travel directly between Portland and The Dalles.

I did not expect to get to the city with my fore sick children and my oldest girl that was sick. I was looking all the time for her to die. I tuck my seat in the canoe by her and held her up and the same at nite when I came to the cascade falls. I had to make portage of 3 miles. I put my sick girl in a blanket and packed her & only rested once that day. We maid the portage with the help of my fore Indians....

Samuel Parker - Mid-October, 1845

For those not opting for the water route, the Barlow Trail of 1846 permitted an alternate path over the Cascades — through a country as the emigrants had never before seen. The route led south from The Dalles, through dry, rolling country until it reached light stands of oak intermingled with large yellow pine along the eastern flank of the mountains. The dry Columbia Plain gave way to the wet and cold of the Cascades. The slopes steepened and the forest became increasingly dense, the trees mightier, as the road climbed up White River to Barlow Pass. Ahead was Mt. Hood towering over 6000 feet above them. The rest of the route to Oregon City was a descent and crossing of the Zigzag and Sandy rivers, then on to the Willamette Valley through a dim, dank forest of giant Douglas-fir, western hemlock, red cedar, and Sitka spruce. The understory was a thick ground cover of moss, bracken fern, and tangles of laurel, vine maple, sallal brush, and devils-club. Stock starved in the forest from lack of feed, or sickened on the laurel; and the emigrants, on their last legs, grew sick from the cold and dampness of persistent fall rains.

We started very early this morning and traveled about fifteen miles over some awful roads, and camped. Many stumps and large boulders in the road. Tonight we camped about two miles past the summit, and about four and one-half miles south of Mount Hood. Very little good grass....

E.W. Conyers - September 19, 1852

We started bright and early this morning for Oregon City, traveling
fourteen miles over good roads and through beautiful valleys, passing
several farmhouses, neatly furnished and painted white that gives an
encouraging appearance to us poor worn-out emigrants....
E.W. Conyers - September 24, 1852

Finally, the oak-covered hills and lush green valleys traversed by the Willamette River welcomed the travelers to their new home. Their journey of nearly 2000 miles was over. Oregon City was their first real sign of civilization since crossing the Missouri and heading out into Indian Territory.

Soon the settlements of Linn City, Portland, Milwaukie, and Salem sprung up. Here they spent the winter months waiting for signs of spring before moving out across the Willamette Valley to stake a claim, unsheath the ax, and sink the plow to start life anew. There was time to rest, look for a job to replenish the empty poke sack, and, at last, a chance to finish diaries about their westward adventure and their new beginning in country surrounded by wilderness. It was time to write a letter home, and so it was with Lucia Lorain Williams.

A Letter Home

While on the trail, Lucia had written a letter to her mother and paid a mountain man to deliver it to Fort Laramie. He evidently took the money and cast the letter aside. So, shortly after her arrival in the Willamette Valley in the fall of 1851, Lucia wrote another letter to her mother, describing the family's entire journey from Findlay, Ohio to Oregon.

Fortunately the letter was kept in the family and a copy transcribed around the turn of the century. It is a rare find and wonderful illustration of the common experiences shared by emigrants traveling westward during the heyday of the Oregon Trail.

To use the letter for publication, editorial license has been taken with paragraphing, abbreviations, and punctuation to assist in clarity and ease of reading; otherwise, the letter is complete as transcribed from the original. Strangely, the letter ends very abruptly, and there is no evident reason for this, unless the ending and signature were left off in the transcription.

Lucia came west with her husband, Elijah (often refered to as Mr. Williams or "W"), and four children — Richard, George, Little John, and Helen. The family left Ohio in early spring to travel by ox team over the trapper-missionary-Mormon route following the Platte River westward until crossing over the Platte River. Then they traveled the Oregon Trail to the Cascade Mountains of Oregon, and the Barlow Road over the mountains to reach Milwaukie, Oregon on the 3rd of September.

On the sixteenth, Lucia began her letter home.

September 16, 1851

Dear Mother,

We have been living in Oregon about two weeks, all of us except little John, and him we left twelve miles this side of Green River. He was killed instantly by falling from a wagon and the wheels running over his head.

After passing the desert and Green River we came to a place of feed and laid by a day for the purpose of recruiting our teams. On the morning of the 29 June we started on. John rode on the wagon driven by Edwin Fellows. We had not proceeded more than 2 miles before word came for us to turn back — we did so but found him dead. The oxen had taken fright, from a horse that had been tied behind the wagon preceding this owned by a young man that Mr. Williams had told a few minutes before to leave, and turned off the road. Two other teams ran also.

John was sitting in the back of the wagon, but as soon as the cattle commenced to run, he went to the front and caught hold of the driver who held him as long as he could, but he was frightened and did not possess presence of mind enough to give him a little send which perhaps would have saved him.

Poor little fellow! We could do nothing for him, he was beyond our reach and O! How suddenly!

One half hour before we had left him in health as lively as a lark, and then to find him so breathless so soon was awful. I cannot describe to you our feelings.

We buried him there by the roadside, on the right side of the road, about ½ mile before we crossed the Fontonelle, a little stream. We had his grave covered with stones to protect it from wild beasts, and a board with his name and age. If any of our friends come through I wish that they would find his grave and if it needs, repair it.

Helen had been sick nearly all the way and at the time that John died she was getting a little better so that she could get round a little. It was impressed upon my mind that we were not all to get through, but I thought it would be Helen that we should leave, for she was continually sick. We think she had the scarlet fever on the road the night that we passed Ft. Laramie. She was very sick and came out with a fine rash accompanied with a high fever. She would not be satisfied unless I was rubbing her all the time; her throat was sore and she vomited blood several times. After she had partially recovered, the skin came off her hands and feet and from off her body in scales. After recovering she was tolerable healthy and enjoyed herself well. She could talk to the Indians and throw the lariat with a great deal of glee.

An old squaw and a young one with a papoose came and sat on one side of my fire, the papoose tied to a board. They were Snakes and commenced talking to Helen. She would jabber back and laugh, then they would talk and laugh, until they got into quite a spree. The mother of the papoose wanted to swap her papoose for mine but I told her "no swap." I believe she would have done it as she seemed quite eager to trade.

After we passed Ft. Laramie I wrote a letter home and sent it to the Ft. by a mountaineer calling himself a mailcarrier, but have since learned that he was an imposter and that there were others in pursuit of him. As you may not have received that I will mention some things over again concerning our journey. After crossing the Missouri our company was so large that we separated—making two, one bound for Oregon, and the other via Salt Lake. In our company were 14 wagons and 2 carriages, one baptist preacher from Iowa, one family from near Norwalk, Ohio—the gentleman's name was Lockhart. Mrs. L's sister accompanied them.

The ladies are sisters to Hannah Adams' stepmother. Also there were Judge Olney from Iowa and two other families, one a widow with five small children. They elected Mr. Williams Captain in which honourable office he served until we crossed the Blue Mountains and were out of danger from Indians.

The first tribe that we passed through was the Omaha. They are a beggarly set. Next came the Pawnee and they are the tallest, strongest, and most savage, also the noblest looking of any of the tribes that I have seen while we were camped at Shell Creek. Several of them came and staid with us—they were nearly starved. Their hunting excursion the fall previous had not proved successful and most of their warriors, some 300, had then gone onto disputed territory, between them and the Sioux, to hunt. The day previous to our arrival at Shell Creek the Pawnees had taken two cows from a company, exacting them as pay for passing through their country and the captain, being afraid, dared not refuse. They wanted some cattle of us but did not get any.

Smith came up and camped with us and Jon Williams
company from Illinois, also several other companies who all united
in constructing a bridge over the creek.

The next day, 13 May, about noon, companies commenced crossing some 80 wagons, all in a heap. The bridge was constructed of brush with logs on top. We swam the cattle and crossed a little before sundown, went through a sea of water onto an island and camped without wood. In the morn the wind arose and blew the carriage over with Helen and myself in it — Mr. W standing upon the wheel to keep it down. However, they got us out without serious injury to us, but the carriage top was broken short off, for the wheels stood uppermost for two hours. I never saw it blow harder. Mr. Lockhart's wagon started off towards the river and three men could not stop it until they succeeded in running the tongue into the ground. Mrs. Olney's bonnet, a leghorn was blown off the boiler to my stove, tin pans, hats and pillows, buckets, etc., etc. — nothing recovered but the pillows belonging to Mr. L and to Captain. All our cattle gone but we succeeded in finding all but one cow that was given to Mr. W by the owner of the Ferry on the missouri; she was an excellent cow and I suppose that the Pawnees got her.

Arrived at Loup Fork on the 15th - a perfect jam - the ferryman was a half-breed. While here we saw the Pawnee hunters returning loaded with buffalo meat half dried. It was thought that they had some 8000 lbs on their ponies. After crossing Loup Fork we passed the first grave, and from that on until we passed all the roads turning off to California there was not a day that we did not pass one or more.

21 May — we had one of the worst storms that I ever read of. It beggars all description — thunder, lightning, hail, rain, and wind. Hailstones so large that they knocked a horse onto his knees. The driver got out and held the oxen by the heads for they showed a disposition to run. Most of our things were completely soaked, so the next day we stopped and dried up. It was the last hard storm that we had.

On the 23rd we came to a creek that overflowed its banks, Elm Creek. The water was some 20 feet deep but not very wide. They fell a tree over the creek and packed the loading, put our wagons into the water with a rope attached to the tongue, and swam them across. While there, two strangers on horseback came to our camp — one, a Mr. Kinny who had lost a hundred head of cattle in a stampede occasioned by the severest storm he said that he ever witnessed. He was some days ahead of us and had run out of provisions. We gave him his dinner and supplied him with sugar, coffee, bread, ect. while he would be looking for his cattle. On the 28th we came up with Kinny; he had found one third of his stock. While here we had buffalo meat. We did not like it very well as it is much coarser than beef. We saw herds of them. The antelope, and this country abounds with them, is most excellent — also mountain rabbit. Passed several prairie dog village. W and myself went among them but they ran barking to their houses which are holes in the ground. They are as large as a half grown kitten.

31 May — camped near the lone Cedar tree - received visits from seven Sioux Indians prepared supper for them.

June 1 — passed the Sioux village. Their wigwams are made of buffalo skins (the Pawnees were mud). They seemed to be a much wealthier tribe than any that we have yet seen. The squaws were in antelope skins ornamented with beads; the men were also clothed with skin or blankets. They owned a great many ponies. On one of the wigwams were several scalps hung out to dry — taken from the Pawnees — they were friendly.

I saw some beautiful bluffs, apparently not more than ½ mile off, and wished to visit them. W consented to go with me but said that it was further than I anticipated. We walked 4 miles, I should judge, crossing chasms and bluffs before we reached the road and after all did not ascend the one we set out for. Camped by the Platte. No wood but buffalo chips, which we have used for a long time.

4 June — passed Chimmney Rock and camped under Scotts Bluff near two wigwams. They came over to eat with us. I helped to get supper for two Indians. We gave them a knife and fork — they took the knife but refused the forks. They were well dressed in blankets with a hood to come over the head. They were very careful to take all from their plates and tie it up in a corner of their blankets. They belonged to the Cheyennes.

On the 7th we arrived at Ft. Laramie and on the 8th commenced crossing the black hills. Some of them were steep. Laramie Peak to the left covered with snow.

9 June — crossed the red hills and camped by a lake.

17 June — traveled over 20 miles and camped by the Devils hole, or gate. In the morning two young ladies and myself visited it. The rocks on each side were perpendicular, 400 feet high, and the narrowest place was about 3 feet, where Sweetwater came tumbling through. The road leading to it was crooked and thorny, but we found all kinds of beautiful flowers blooming beside the rocks; it was the most sublime spectacle that I ever witnessed. I must not forget to notice Independence Rock which we passed yesterday. I did not ascend it but read several names of friends.

We are in the Sweetwater Mountains which are plentifully besprinkled with snow. The wind which comes from them is very cold—a shawl is not uncomfortable any of the time excepting when the air is still, then it is uncomfortably warm.

Gathered several pounds of Saleratus, very nice, from a lake that had dried up. We have to take particular care that our cattle do not drink at any of these alkali springs and lakes—carcasses of cattle are plenty along here. Crossed Sweetwater seven times and passed the Wind Mountains where it blew a perfect hurricane all the time.

19 June—can see the Rocky Mountains a distance of some 60 miles. The tops were covered with snow, and from there they looked like fleecy clouds. Camped near two snowbanks in a beautiful valley.

22 June—passed between the twin mounds and over the south pass of the Rocky Mountains. We could hardly tell when we were on the summit. The ascent had been so gradual, although we were nearly 8000 feet above the level of the sea. A little to our right are ranges that are covered with snow. Nights and mornings we suffered with cold. Camped at the Pacific Springs.

25 June – After laying by a day on Big Sandy, started on to the desert at about 2 o'clock P.M. – found it a barren sandy plain, no vegetation except some stunted sage. Drove all night. Towards morning found it more hilly until we came down to Green river which was high and rapid. Paid $10 per team for ferriage here. We found several white families living in wigwams. They were Mormons and soon going to Salt Lake. Also some white men having squaws for wives. Snake Indians, the most of their tribe with Mourner their chief, had removed to Bear River a few days previous.

July 1 – crossed Bear River through an Indian village and were guided by them across the water. Passed some traders; paid them toll for crossing a bridge over a slough and Thomas Fork, camped on the latter.

2 July – last night we were awakened by serenaders – five horsemen circled around the carriage singing Araby's Daughter. It was a beautiful starlight night. We were surrounded by bluffs in a little valley, and had on being awakened by their song, seeing their panting steeds and looking around upon the wild country, it seemed as tho we were transported into Arabia. They were beautiful singers from Oregon, said they were exiles from home.

Mr. Williams arose. They sang "Sweet Home" and several others. Invited us to stay and celebrate the 4th. Said they would make us a barbecue but we were anxious to get on and the affliction that we had just suffered unfitted us for such a scene. Jo Williams and company remained.

5 July – came to the Soda Springs about noon. The water oozed up from between the rocks, the surface of which was red as blood. The water was warm. A little farther on we came to the cold spring which was in the bank of Bear River. There were two close together - one in a rock - the water boiled up as it would have done in a cauldron kettle and was very cold. When sweetened it tasted like small beer. I was fond of it, took a canteen full and started on, but the gas escaped soon and was not good. There were two white families at this place. A mile farther and we came to the Steamboat springs where the water rises about 2 feet, foaming from the middle of a rock. The water was soda and warm; the rock was also warm. For several feet around the basin the noise resembled the puffing of a steamboat. Plenty of Snake Indians begging for bread or shirts or any kind of clothing. We could get a pair of moccasins for a bit of bread. At night we camped beyond a pool of soda water which is said not to be good at this place. There were two traders living with squaw wives. I took Helen and called upon them. They were going to Ft. Hall with a band of ponies to sell.

6 July – Lockhart and Rexford, the baptist preacher, remained in camp to recruit their cattle. The rest of us moved on to a creek – plenty of willows for fuel and fish. We bought some salmon trout from an Indian for a couple of pancakes.

8 July – Travelled 20 miles - most of the way sandy, camped on a branch of the Snake, two Indians came into camp. Mr. W made them stay all night as they looked rather suspicious. About midnight one of them arose cautiously and crept in the direction of one of our horses. On seeing the guard was watching him, he laid down a bit before he tried again, but with no better success.

9th July – arrived at Ft. Hall a desolate looking place and filled with thieves. We saw one man emigrant that had lost nine horses. He offered $100 reward. The Indians brought four back. He then offered as much more. The Indians then started again; in all probability they were the ones that took them. The whitemen traders are worse than Indians. We heard of a great many emigrants who had lost horses, and one company who had lost twenty-four head of cattle near this place.

10 July – heard that Lockhart and Rexford wanted us to wait for them. Accordingly, laid by near a pond where was excellent grass. At night they came up, minus two horses. One they recovered, belonging to a hand; the other belonged to Mr. R which he did not recover, making the 2nd that he had lost. The first was taken from him while in Canesville.

11 July – on starting, found that two head of our stock were staggering from the effects of alkali which they had eaten with grass – the ground in some places was white with it, under the grass. Mr. W fed one fat pork and lard and left it with a couple of men. The other, a cow, soon fell. He gave it alcohol and left it at night. The ox was driven in but the cow was dead - the last one that gave milk.

14 July — drove 22 miles; camped on Spring run. An Indian half breed camped within a few rods of us with several horses going to Oregon. On one side of us was quite a patch of rushes 6 feet high. At night there seemed to be considerable fuss in the rushes — a duck was scared up, the mules were frightened and ran the length of their lariat from the rushes — our guard kept a vigilant watch. In the morning one of Indian Dick's horses was gone. His squaw and papooses started on with us but he went in pursuit of his horse.

16 July — Dick the Indian came up. He had recovered his horse, said he traced his horse behind the bluffs where he saw his with three more American horses and three Indians. One of the Snakes shot an arrow at him which he dodged; he then shot another which he also dodged. It was then Dick's turn who fired his rifle loaded with three balls. One of the Indians dropped; the others ran. He then seized his horse and another one and started back but an Indian shot the other horse. Dick belongs to the Nez Perces and hates the Snakes as bad as a whiteman does.

17 July — last night at twilight we had quite a fright. Dick camped by us again. Williams was at his fire when he discovered 4 Indians creeping along the brow of the hill. Dick caught his rifle and ran crouching about 200 yards and fired. One of the Indians hollered in a manner that I never shall forget and they all ran. Our folks ran back to camp for weapons. Those that had no rifles armed themselves with axes, clubs, or any thing that they could get hold of. We did not know but there was a body of them at hand and thought best to be prepared for the worst. We were unfortunately camped near a thick body of willows on the other side of which was a small creek whose banks were rather steep. Mr. W told myself and children to get into a wagon and lay down in the bed. I was preparing to do so when Mrs. Rexford sent for me to come and stay with her. We did so and sat watching the willows for a long time, several times we thought that we heard a splashing and saw an Indian peeping out of the willows. But alas! Sadly, to the disappointment of some who wished to have a round with them, we were not disturbed again.

18 July — traveled about 15 miles over a sandy bottom and camped on the Snake. Descent to water 10 feet — on the opposite bank was a boiling spring. Powell's company camped at the same place. They had a horse stolen last night, fired at an Indian without effect.

20 July — started on to a desert of 25 miles at 2 P.M..
Camped on account of darkness. When the moon arose we again
started. Reached water about 11 A.M. but not before one oxen
had given out entirely. When they let him out of the yoke he reeled

and staggered so that he could not be driven. We then left him 5 miles from water and returned with food and water after which he was able to come to camp. It was a much harder stretch upon our cattle than the first 44 miles, because it was more sandy and warmer also.

28 July — came to the hot springs. There was a little drain or stream running across the road about ½ mile from the spring. It was such beautiful water that several of our company alighted to drink but on a near approach they were satisfied with jerking their heads away. Some complained of burning their lips and those that were at first deceived tried their turn to deceive others. Camped and visited the springs, there were two. We found the water hot enough for cooking. The ground a few feet from the spring was covered with Saleratas, and those of the company who were short of the same replenished their store.

31 July — camped on the Snake. Indians came with salmon to sell. I let them have Helen's apron with a needle and thread and bot salmon enough for several meals. I wish you could eat with us. I certainly never tasted any fowl or fish half so delicious.

August 1 — last night J. Williams came up and camped on one side, on the other a very large Hoosier company. The night before, the H company camped on Rock River, the banks of which are very steep and high. Some five or six Indians came into camp in the morning to sell salmon. While they were trading, one of the Indians jumped on to a valuable horse and made towards the

bluffs. The Indians then showed fight and some twenty or more came up the river bank and dared them to fight. Williams had a man from Illinois that they had shot the week before in the same place where we came so near a fight. This young man was on the last guard, standing before the fire and an Indian shot him through the body. He fell and rose two times, cried "O God! I am shot!" Think of leaving him at Ft. Boise.

2 August – reached Fort Boise. Quite a pretty place situated on the other side of the Snake; did not visit it.

5 August – W's company came up. That young man was considered to be dying. He had hopes of getting well - poor fellow. I did not go to see him.

6 August – camped on Burnt river. W's company came up. The young man is dead and buried. He had one brother with him.

7 August – came to Powder river. The sand and mud was full of shining particles which some took to be gold. There were some so eager to wash gold that they could not eat. We got some specimens.

Camped in one of the lovliest valleys in the world called Grand Round. It resembled an enchanted valley, as we wound around the hill before descending into it. Found plenty of Cayuse Indians.

10 August — moved at the foot of the Blue Mountains. Paid an Indian three shirts for passing over a few miles of new road and avoiding a hill. Plenty of pine timber. Camped at the first creek — no feed. A gentleman from Puget Sound, Oregon staid with us. Going to meet his wife, from whom he had been absent three years. An Indian also to whom I gave supper. He ate a plate of beans, and one of bread, an apple dumpling, meat etc., etc..

11 August — Powell's daughter was brought into camp dead. We passed them at noon and inquired for her. They thought she was better. She left a husband and two children, the youngest a few weeks old. She was confined on the road. Powell is a baptist preacher. In his company are 12 wagons, all connected except two. Bought potatoes and peas of Cayuse squaws. This tribe dress like white people.

13 August — parted into three companies on account of grass being scarce — are out of danger from Indians now. Two Indians nooned with us. One of them showed how he had killed a Snake Indian, his arrow was bloody. Told where he had shot him and how he tore off the scalp. I could not help but shudder — we are alone.

14 August — camped on the Umatilla. Found traders - one old gentleman married to a young squaw. She called at the carriage. I took Helen and visited her wigwam, also several others. We found a Mr. Johnson from Iowa, Presbyterian preacher. He had been laying by for a few days in order to recruit his cattle and in hopes to hear from his cattle that went off in a stampede with Kenny's. He has a wife and several children - two young women grown - appear well.

17 August—camped on John Days river.

25 August—started on to the Cascade Mountains—bad road. Camped on a muddy creek. No feed but plenty of browse - maple and alder.

26 August—left an ox. Commenced raining - cold, very cold. We are near Mt. Hood whose top is covered with snow and above the clouds. Two other lofty peaks, one on each side of Mt. Hood are equally as white and apparently as tall. Towards night found a patch of bunch grass - turned out - but the cattle would not eat it. Yoked up again and started on. Arrived within a mile of the prairie. Several bad hills to descend. I took Helen and walked—got mired. W had gone ahead to find a camp. Word soon came for him to come back to the carriage. One of the wheels needed repairing. Could get no further. Unhitched the mules and oxen and left the wagons on the other side of the slough—drove them to the prairie. It was raining and I could not see to return to the wagons so kept on to where there was several companies camped.

I was cold and wet. Helen was not well. I drew near a fire and seated myself on the root of a tree.

I looked around and discovered two families that had traveled with us a few days. Their names were Allen and Sanders, Mrs. Sanders was the old man's daughter. They shook hands with me and sat down to their supper, never inviting me. Helen was crying for bread, but I tried to quiet her. Soon a lady from another wagon came to me, gave me a seat before the fire, and went to get me some supper. Mr. W came up at that time and thinking that I was going to fare hard, asked Mrs. Woodard to give me some supper. Said he would pay them. They gave me a cup of tea and some bread, ect., but my heart was full and I could not eat. The husband of this other lady, a fine looking man, came up and introduced himself as Mr. Chandler. We had often heard of them on the route. He is a baptist preacher, formerly president of some college in Indiana and going to Oregon City to found some college or school. They are fine people. Mrs. Allen let us have a tent cloth and pillow to make our bed in the rain, but Mrs. Chandler went to work and made us as comfortable as she could under a tree. It rained all night and W got up before day and made a fire close by the bed. Mrs. C gave us breakfast. The next day we were able to return their kindness in some measure. Their horses gave out and could not pull their carriage. We helped them up several hills – took Mrs. C and two children into our wagon. They are Vermonters - Allens are from the reserve.

27 August – I cannot describe these mountains; they have been a scene of suffering. The snow set in next month and falls to the depth of 50 feet. The road is strewed with the bones of cattle, horses, wagons, yokes, and in short a little of everything. Descended on hill where we had to tie trees behind our wagons. Crossed Laurel hill, the worst hill of all. I never could give you a description if I should write all night, so will close my narrative soon.

September 1 – I camped within a mile of a house. Bought some potatoes at $1 per bushel. Had several calls from white men.

2 September — came in sight of a house. Helen clapped her hands, laughed and called me to see. It was a long log house with a stick chimney at one end. Soon we saw another house painted white. She then changed her mind, called that a house and the log one a steam bot. "Ma Ma will we go in and live in that house and see there is chickens and pigs?"

3 September — arrived at Milwaukie went into a house to live again, the first one that I had been in since we crossed the Missouri. Helen was nearly wild with joy - did not want to camp out again.

27 September —you will see from the date that I have been a good while writing. I cannot tell you much about the country as I have seen nought but this place which is situated in the Willamette. Steamboats and vessels from the salt water come here but cannot go to Oregon City at all times. We are eight miles below the city and six from Portland and has the best harbor in the world. It is eighteen months old —has three taverns, three stores - provisions from 50¢ to $1, chickens $1, wheat $1 per bushel, beef is 18¢ per pound. Labor is high, though not as high as formerly -from $2 to $10. A girl can get $1 per day. Most of the house girls, however, are men and boys. Girls are foolish that they do not come to Oregon to marry. There is no end to bachelor establishments - several in this place who board themselves and others hire a cook.

Tell Mrs. Mariam that I have a rich merchant picked out for her, Jane Wilson also. The soil is very productive. They raise three crops from once sowing cabbage three years from one stump. I saw some stumps the other day that had five heads on one stalk.

Our stoves have not come yet. Mr. Smith is expected daily. It is a great place to make money — everything will count. I could have taken a school this winter from $5 to $8 a quarter per scholar but would not. Sold one set of harness for $50 that had been used considerable. One wagon for $150.

Oregon City — 1846

Ezra Meeker retracing the Oregon Trail

In Closing

Of the half million pioneers who traveled the Oregon Trail, many, if not most, were exceptional people. But one man in particular stands out, exemplifying the true Western pioneer. His name was Ezra Meeker.

Up to his dying breath in 1928, he was committed to the memorialization of America's greatest trail. Without question, he knew it better than any man, dead or alive, for he had traversed it with his wife and child in 1852, his own mother was buried somewhere along it, and his brother was drowned in the Sweetwater River just above Devils Gate. In 1906, at the age of 76, he retraced his journey with ox team and covered wagon to reblaze the trail and to enlist public support and involvement in monumenting it. In 1910 he started on another 2½ year jaunt to relocate and map sixteen hundred miles of the historic highway. And in 1924 he made his last trip over the trail, this time by airplane, to further plead his case and publicize his cause.

To Ezra Meeker, the Oregon Trail was symbolic of the heroism, the patriotism, the vision, and the sacrifice of pioneers who won the West for America. He could visualize but one tribute to them worthy of these sacrifices—to restore the old "Lost Trail" by marking it for all time, reclaiming and preserving the historic spots along the way.

It is interesting to note the functioning of government bureaucracy; it was 24 years after his meeting with President Theodore Roosevelt that Congress, in 1930, authorized commemoration of the heroism of the pioneers who traversed the Oregon Trail to the Far West, with President Herbert Hoover proclaiming a nation-wide commemoration in celebration of the 100th anniversary of Ezra Meeker's birth.

Then 48 years passed before Congress, in 1978, passed the National Trails System Act providing for the preservation and monumentation of historic trails, and public use for the good of future generations.

It is our intent, with the publishing of "A Letter Home", to pay tribute to the Ezra Meeker spirit wherever it may be found today. It is that spirit which will continue to promote public awareness to Ezra's lifelong cause: remembering, reverently, the Oregon Trail and its critical historical importance to this Nation.

Historical Notes

Chronological History of the Oregon Trail

1792 - American Captain Robert Gray discovers and names the Columbia River.

1803 - Louisiana Purchase brings the United States territory to the summit of the Rocky Mountains.

1804 - Americans Lewis and Clark start an expedition to seek an overland route to the Pacific.

1811 - Pacific Fur Company establishes Fort Astoria on the Columbia River.

1812 - Robert Stuart and party of Astorians travel east and discover South Pass of the Rockies.

1812 - War with Great Britain.

1818 - The United States and Great Britain sign a treaty for joint occupancy of the Oregon Country.

1819 - Treaty with Spain fixes the southern boundary of the Oregon Country.

1821 - August 10th — Missouri admitted as 24th state to the Union.

1825 - Fort Vancouver dedicated by the Hudson's Bay Company.

1830 - First wagon caravan of Smith-Jackson-Sublette travels the Oregon Trail route, to rendezvous.

1832 - Captain Bonneville travels with first loaded wagons over South Pass.

1832 - Nathaniel Wyeth travels to the Columbia River on his first expedition.

1834 - Nathaniel Wyeth, on his second expedition, establishes Fort Hall on Snake River.

1834 - Methodist minister Jason Lee establishes the Willamette Mission.

1836 - Whitman party brings a two-wheel cart as far as Fort Hall. Protestant Whitman Mission established at Waiilatpu.

1839 - First group of settlers, the 18 man Peoria Party, arrives in Oregon.

1841 - Fort John (Fort Laramie) built on the North Platte River by the American Fur Company. Other fur trading posts were established here as early as 1834.

1841 - The Bidwell-Bartleson party of 80 emigrants are guided westward by Thomas Fitzpatrick.

1841 - Jim Bridger establishes Fort Bridger trading post. Wyoming's oldest permanent settlement.

1842 - The White wagon train with 112 emigrants travels as far as Fort Hall with wagons.

1843 - First mass migration of settlers westward...over 1000 emigrants, 120 wagons, and several thousand head of loose stock travel over the Oregon Trail.

1843 - First provisional government in the Oregon Country established at Champoeg.

1845 - Over 3000 emigrants and 500 wagons head for Oregon.

1846 - Treaty with Great Britain establishes the Oregon boundary at 49 degrees, north.

1846 - Estimated 2000 emigrants on the Oregon Trail - including the ill-fated Donner Party.

1847 - Over 3500 emigrants travel westward—Mormon Trail established with 144 traveling to the Great Salt Lake Valley.

1847 - Fort Childs established on the Platte River—named Fort Kearney in 1848.

1847 - Whitman massacre at Waiilatpu. The Cayuse Indian War follows.

1848 - Oregon Territory established.

1848 - Over 12,000 emigrants travel westward.

1848 - Gold discovered at Sutter's Ranch in California.

1849 - California Gold Rush is on—over 20,00 emigrants and gold seekers head westward.

1850 - Donation Land Claim Law enacted. The Rogue Indian War begins.

1850 - September 9—California admitted as the 31st state.

1852 - Over 50,000 emigrants travel the Oregon Trail.

1859 - February 14—Oregon admitted as the 33rd state.

1861 - January 29—Kansas admitted as the 34th state.

1864 - October 31—Nevada admitted as the 36th state.

1867 - March 1—Nebraska admitted as the 37th state.

1869 - First transcontinental railroad completed - linking East to West by rail.

1889 - November 8—Montana admitted as the 41st state.

1889 - November 11—Washington admitted as the 42nd state.

1890 - July 3—Idaho admitted as the 43rd state.

1890 - July 10—Wyoming admitted as the 44th state.

1896 - January 4—Utah admitted as the 45th state.

1906 - Ezra Meeker retraces his 1852 journey to monument the Oregon Trail.

1923 - Ezra Meeker founds the Oregon Trail Memorial Association and is elected first president.

1978 - Congress passed the National Trails System Act.

Ezra Meeker

Ezra Meeker was born December 29, 1830 near Huntsville, Ohio where his father was engaged in the milling trade.

Ezra gained experience early in life by driving four yoke of oxen for twenty-five cents a day, and then switched to the printing trade at the young age of fourteen.

In October of 1851 he took Eliza Jane for a wife, and they headed to Eddyville, Iowa to become farmers. After a severe winter in Iowa and the promise of 320 acres of free land in Oregon, they headed west in spring of 1852 with a month-old baby, one wagon, two yoke of steers, and three cows. The family arrived in Portland on the 1st day of October, and shortly thereafter headed north to settle in the Puyallup Valley of Washington where Ezra founded the town of Puyallup, Washington.

After a lifetime of helping to develop the country west of the Cascades, Ezra spent his waning years committed to relocating and symbolizing the Oregon Trail.

In 1906, at the age of 76, he set out with ox team and wagon to retrace the old Oregon Trail from The Dalles to the Missouri, then continued on to Washington D.C. to plead his cause with President Theodore Roosevelt.

In 1910 he again set out to relocate and map sixteen hundred miles of the historic highway—indeed a strenuous task for an eighty-year-old.

In 1923 he founded and was elected first president of the Oregon Trail Memorial Association to continue his efforts to bring recognition to the historic trail.

To further publicize his cause he made his last trip over the Oregon Trail in 1924, this time by airplane, when he rode in an open cockpit from Vancouver, Washington to the Missouri River. Then he continued on to the nation's capitol to meet with President Calvin Coolidge.

Ezra Meeker never saw his goal truly accomplished within his lifetime, although since his death on December 3, 1928, efforts to fulfill his dream are slowly continuing.

Lucia Lorain Williams　　　　　　*Elijah Williams*

Lucia, the last of seven children, was born in 1815 to Rev. Henry and Margaret Bigelow of Middletown, Vermont.

On April 23, 1845, in Findlay, Ohio, she was married to Elijah Williams, a widower with three boys.

The couple left Findlay for Oregon in 1851. With them were Mr. William's three sons — Richard, 15; George, 12; and John, 11 — and their daughter, Helen Lorain, 4.

The family traveled in company with thirteen other wagons and two carriages — all bound for Oregon over the Mormon Trail-Oregon Trail route — and arrived in Milwaukie, Oregon on September 3rd of the same year.

Shortly thereafter, the family settled permanently in Salem, Oregon where a son, Emmet Bigalow, was born in 1853.

Elijah left a law practice in Ohio when he moved West with his family. He did not continue his profession in Oregon, but his sons Richard and Emmet engaged as partners and practiced law in Portland, Oregon.

Daughter Helen married M.A. Stratton and resided in Oregon City, and son George was commissioned a Major in the Civil War.

Lucia lived the rest of her life in Salem until her death on the 22nd of May, 1874.

—◇◆◇◆◇◆◇—

Listing of Illustrations —

Original Photography by Gildemeister   ## Original Art by Don Gray

The Elkhorn Range of the Blue Mountains — 1975 *(p. 52-53)*...Powder Valley of northeast Oregon.

The Trail over the Blue Mountains — *(p.55)...Ezra Meeker Collection.*

Blue Mountain Summit — 1985 *(p. 56)*...West of Emigrant Springs.

Well Spring — 1984 *(p. 58)*...Along Oregon's Columbia Plain.

Nearing Journey's End — *(p. 60-61)...Author's file.*

The Columbia River — 1984 *(p. 62)*...River Gorge at Cascade Locks.

Mt. Hood — 1984 *(p. 64)*.

Willamette Reflections — 1987 *(p. 66)*...Mt. Hood and the Willamette River.

A Letter Home — 1987 *(p. 68)...Pencil Art, 11½"x13".*

Passing Through — 1987 *(p. 70-71)...Acrylic, 15"x32½".*

Bridge Builders — 1987 *(p. 76)...Acrylic, 18½"x19".*

Camp at Scotts Bluff — 1987 *(p. 80-81)...Acrylic, 15"x32½".*

Horseback Singers — 1987 *(p. 84)...Acrylic, 12"x18".*

Alkali — 1987 *(p. 88)...Acrylic, 15"x16'.*

Across the Desert — 1987 *(p. 92-93)...Acrylic, 12½"x27½".*

Along the Umatilla — 1987 *(p. 97)...Acrylic, 9½"x18½".*

A Night on the Barlow Road — 1987 *(p. 99)...Acrylic, 15"x16".*

Log House — 1987 *(p. 102)...Acrylic, 15"x16".*

Oregon City — 1846 — 1987 *(p. 105)...Pencil, 10"x13".*
    From a painting by Henry Warre.

Ezra Meeker retracing the Oregon Trail — 1906 *(p. 106)...Meeker Collection.*

Lucia Lorain and Elijah Williams — *(p. 113)...Helen Althaus Collection.*

Writer & Photographer
Jerry Gildemeister

Jerry's long-time interest in the American West drew him to the Blue Mountains of Northeast Oregon over a quarter century ago to begin his profession in forestry. After a two-year stint in the 82nd Airborne and the U.S. Army Special Services he returned to Union, Oregon to continue with the U.S. Forest Service and start a secondary career in photography. He and his wife Cathy now share this career which has since expanded into full-time consultation, photography, design, and publishing. They live and work in their studio-home which is located in the foothills of the Wallowa Mountains near Union.

In addition to publishing under the Bear Paw imprint, Jerry has designed and photo-illustrated the Bear Wallow's Limited Edition Printings of *RENDEZVOUS*, *TRACES*, *WHERE ROLLS THE OREGON*, and *A LETTER HOME*.

In concurrence with their publishing endeavors, Jerry and Cathy also coordinate a variety of photographic, design, graphic arts, marketing, and publishing services for those seeking personal commitment and quality in design and production.

Artist
Don Gray

After a brief stint teaching high school art classes, Don Gray returned to his native northeast Oregon in 1971 to begin painting full-time.

Since then he has exhibited in museums and galleries in most of the Western States, as well as New York and Chicago. His paintings have found their way into many collections, both public and private.

In addition to *A LETTER HOME*, Don has illustrated other Bear Wallow limited printings of *RENDEZVOUS*, and *TRACES*, plus several other books of poetry and stories.

Don lives on a small acreage near Union, Oregon with his wife Brenda and children Heather, Melissa, and Jared.

The Bear Wallow Story

The Bear Wallow Publishing Company was formed in 1976 with a commitment to help preserve our Western Heritage and offer excellence in publication. From the beginning we have strived to carve a niche in the giant world of publishing by developing a distinctive style of design, richly blending illustration with text, and sparing little to offer one-of-a-kind Limited Printings suitable for any coffee table or to be cherished in any library. Our goal is to make history interesting and entertaining to readers of all ages, while preserving some of our great Western Heritage before it is lost forever.

Co-Publisher *Cathy Gildemeister*

Our first endeavor under the sign of the Bear Paw was *RENDEZVOUS*, a lavishly illustrated history of Northeast Oregon depicting the change in the country since the coming of the whiteman. To continue our pledge, we produced *TRACES* in 1980 — the stories of the last still-living Oregon Trail Pioneers who came West by covered wagon. Original art and photography were created to blend with the storyline. In 1985 we released another collector's edition with the debut of *WHERE ROLLS THE OREGON*, the rich history of the Oregon Country — from discovery to settlement, taken from the diaries and other writings of sea voyagers, trappers, mountain men, and pioneers. Color photography was used vividly throughout the volume to re-create the mood of the countryside in the early 1800s.

Our future plans revolve around our pledge to produce distinctive, one-of-a-kind Limited Edition Printings, continuing our style of blending illustration with story, while maintaining excellence in publication.

— Credits —

Writing, photography and design —
   by Gildemeister.
Artwork by Don Gray.
Typesetting by Gildemeister.
Color prints of artwork for color separation, copy/
restoration of historic photographs, and prints for
halftone reproduction by Cathy Gildemeister.
Color Separations by —
   Cascade Color of Portland, Oregon.

Text paper, Midtec Lithofect Suede, and end
papers, French Paper Company Parchtone Cover
supplied by —
   Fraser Paper Company of Portland, Oregon.
Printing of book and end papers by —
   The Irwin-Hodson Co. of Portland, Oregon.
The book was bound by —
   Lincoln and Allen Co. of Portland, Oregon.
Production coordination by —
   Jerry and Cathy Gildemeister.

Library of Congress Cataloging-in-Publication Data

Gildemeister, Jerry, 1934 —

Writing, photography, & design: J. Gildemeister.
Art Illustration: Don Gray.
Includes Historical Data and Illustration Index.

Summary: The early history of the Oregon Trail with
personal diary accounts and complete letter of the journey
westward in the mid-1800s.....illustrated with original
art and photographic illustrations plus selected historic
photographs.

A Letter Home

1. Oregon Trail. 2. Oregon Trail — Pictorial works.
3. Overland journeys to the Pacific. 4. Overland journeys
to the Pacific — Pictorial works. 5. West (U.S.) —
Description and travel — 184-1860. 6. West (U.S.) —
Description and travel — 1843-1860 — Views.
   I. Gray, Don, 1948-   II. Title.
   F597.G45   1987   917.8'04   87-1151
                ISBN0-936376-04-X

— Other Publications by The Bear Wallow —

RENDEZVOUS, First Printing © *1978 (sold out)* . . . . ISBN 0-936376-00-7.
RENDEZVOUS, Second Printing © *1978* . . . . ISBN 0-936376-01-5.
TRACES, Limited Printing © *1980 (sold out)* . . . . ISBN 0-936376-02-3.
WHERE ROLLS THE OREGON, Limited Edition © *1985* . . . ISBN 0-936376-03-1.

In Parting

I wish to extend special thanks to Katharine McCanna who brought Lucia Lorain Williams' letter to our attention, and to Helen Althaus, great-grandaughter of Lucia, who so graciously consented to its use for this book. Also, a note of thanks to Randall Wagner, Director of the Wyoming Travel Commission, for providing a copy of the E. W. Conyers diary of 1852, and to Jack Evans, Director of Eastern Oregon State College Libraries, for the Ezra Meeker writings which were used in the research for this project.

And, finally, I am indebted to my wife, partner, and co-worker — Cathy, whose long hours of work, patient understanding, and sheer endurance made this special project possible.

Jerry Gildemeister

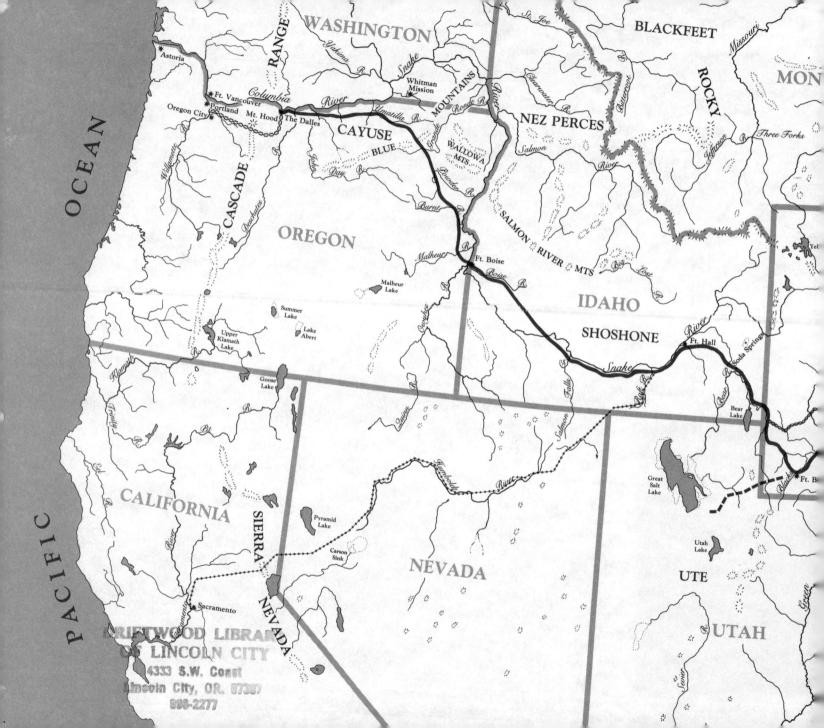

PACIFIC OCEAN

WASHINGTON

RANGE

BLACKFEET

ROCKY

MON

Astoria

Columbia River

Ft. Vancouver

Oregon City

Portland   Mt. Hood   The Dalles

CAYUSE

Yakima

Snake

Whitman Mission

MOUNTAINS

Ronde R.

Umatilla R.

NEZ PERCES

St. Joe

Missouri

Clearwater R.

Bitterroot

Three Forks

CASCADE

Willamette

BLUE

Day R.

John

Grande

WALLOWA MTS

Powder R.

Salmon

River

Jefferson R.

OREGON

Deschutes

Burnt R.

Malheur R.

Ft. Boise

SALMON RIVER MTS

Big

Lost R.

Malheur Lake

Boise R.

IDAHO

SHOSHONE

River

Ft. Hall

Soda Springs

Summer Lake

Owyhee R.

Upper Klamath Lake

Lake Abert

Goose Lake

Snake

Salmon Falls

Bear R.

Bear Lake

Klamath R.

Trinity R.

CALIFORNIA

SIERRA

Humboldt River

Great Salt Lake

Ft. B

Blackf

El R.

Pyramid Lake

Carson Sink

NEVADA

Utah Lake

UTE

River

Sacramento

NEVADA

UTAH

Green

Sevier